WALKING BY
FAITH
~ through a ~
PANDEMIC

Also by
Richard E. Simmons III

REFLECTIONS ON THE EXISTENCE OF GOD
A Series of Essays

THE REASON FOR LIFE
Why Did God Put Me Here?

THE POWER OF A HUMBLE LIFE
Quiet Strength in an Age of Arrogance

WISDOM
Life's Great Treasure

SEX AT FIRST SIGHT
Understanding the Modern Hookup Culture

A LIFE OF EXCELLENCE
Wisdom for Effective Living

THE TRUE MEASURE OF A MAN
*How Perceptions of Success,
Achievement & Recognition Fail Men in Difficult Times*

RELIABLE TRUTH
The Validity of the Bible in an Age of Skepticism

SAFE PASSAGE
Thinking Clearly About Life & Death

REMEMBERING THE FORGOTTEN GOD
The Search for Truth in the Modern World

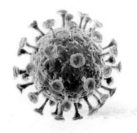

WALKING BY FAITH
~ *through a* ~
PANDEMIC

Experiencing

God's Peace

RICHARD E. SIMMONS III

Walking By Faith Through A Pandemic

Copyright © 2020 by Richard E. Simmons III
All rights reserved.
This book is protected under the copyright laws
of the United States of America. This book may not be copied
or reprinted for commercial gain or profit.
Union Hill is the book publishing imprint of The Center for
Executive Leadership, a 501(c)3 nonprofit organization.

Union Hill Publishing
200 Union Hill Drive, Suite 200
Birmingham, AL 35209

www.richardesimmons3.org

1 2 3 4 5 6 7 8 9 10

Printed in the United States of America

TABLE OF CONTENTS

INTRODUCTION 3

CHAPTER 1
Understanding Fear 5

CHAPTER 2
Preparing the Way 13

CHAPTER 3
What We Need To Know About God 17

CHAPTER 4
Does God Use Suffering Purposefully? 27

CHAPTER 5
Responding to the Storms of Life 35

CHAPTER 6
A Grateful Heart 39

CHAPTER 7
Acceptance 43

CHAPTER 8
One Day at a Time 53

CHAPTER 9
Experiencing God's Peace 59

EPILOGUE 67

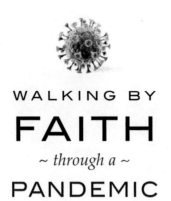

WALKING BY
FAITH
~ through a ~
PANDEMIC

INTRODUCTION

VERY EARLY in 2020 we began to hear rumblings of a threatening virus breaking out on the other side of the world. January 21 marked the day of the first Covid diagnosis in the United States. February 2 global air travel became restricted. March 11 the World Health Organization declared COVID-19 a global pandemic.

Since then our world has become a place of masks, hand sanitizer, shutdowns, work from home, virtual learning, social distancing, testing, quarantining, curbside pickups, zoom meetings, drive-by birthdays and weddings. Not to mention the rampant unemployment, business closings, evictions, hunger and mounting debt.

Back in the spring, I gave a series of presentations on walking by faith through this pandemic. It was very well received yet I recognized a host of people were still struggling.

It struck me that most of the natural disasters we face have a beginning and an end. Once they are over, the damage is assessed and the rebuilding begins. There seems to be at the very least some degree of certainty about the future, and what it might look like.

This however is not the case with the coronavirus pandemic. We do not know when or how this is going to end and consequently are forced to admit that we are not in control. Furthermore, if you are in a high risk category, whether by age or an underlying health condition, you face daily the possibility of serious illness or even death.

This booklet is to help you, the reader, experience peace in the times we are living. I hope and pray you will be blessed by it!

CHAPTER 1

Understanding Fear

"People have always been stressed. It is simply part of living. There has always been change to cope with. There have always been economic problems, and people have always battled depression. It is the nature of life to have its ups and downs—so why all the fuss?

I'm not the one who's making the fuss; I'm only writing about it. I'm only being honest about what I see around me. I sit in my examining room and listen. Then I report what I hear. Something is wrong. People are tired and frazzled. People are anxious and depressed. People don't have the time to heal anymore. There is a psychic instability in our day that prevents peace from implanting itself very firmly in the human spirit. And despite the skeptics, this instability is not the same old nemesis recast in a modern role."

These sobering words were written well before the COVID-19 pandemic, by Dr. Richard Swenson, in his best-selling book, *Margin*. As a physician in cultural medicine, his research led him to conclude something has changed in the lives of modern people. There seems to be a real instability in our land, where finding peace is more difficult. As we face this virus of epic proportion, how are people living amidst so much uncertainty and fear?

Fear typically involves future events that have the potential to turn out badly. It begins in our thinking, stirring up anxious emotions, which are often difficult to extinguish until there is a foreseeable solution. Fear can be easily amplified in our minds when run unchecked in our imagination, often leading to the proverbial phrase, "mountain out of a mole hill."

Fear and the Coronavirus

Several years ago I made a presentation on dealing with fear, stress and anxiety. My research concludes that most of our fears can be broken down into four main categories, with most fears related to issues where we have no control. It's of no surprise that the COVID-19 pandemic falls into all four categories.

* **Business and Financial Life**

There is plenty we can do to build success in our business and financial life, yet with the coronavirus, we are quickly learning our lives are not bulletproof. We have little—if any—control when it comes to the economy.

This virus has disrupted our economic system, shut down businesses, caused massive unemployment and created tremendous uncertainty over what the future holds —which is what creates our fears.

Many businesses that have temporarily closed will never reopen. Banks face the possibility of mass defaults on loans. Rental property owners fear tenants won't be able to pay rent. General contractors are finding awarded jobs to be suspended or cancelled. The consequential ripple effect impacts us all.

One of the greatest fears many people face today, even before COVID 19, is whether they will have the financial resources to retire without running out of money. The virus has only amplified this concern.

✶ The Well-Being of Our Families and Loved Ones

The coronavirus has induced us to worry about our loved ones, particularly those considered high risk. Concerns for our children's success have grown, too.

Parents experience tremendous anxiety over their children's future. Will they be able to return to school in the fall? What about employment? As one father mentioned, his daughter had just graduated from college with a wonderful job lined up, but the position was eliminated. Not only was she devastated, but the father was as well.

It strikes me how parents easily deify their children's lives and success. They agonize over how their children's lives will turn out, and the pandemic's uncertain fallout only makes matters worse.

✶ What Are People Going to Think?

One of the greatest fears people struggle with is what people think about them. Often, they aren't even aware of it. Ultimately, it's a fear of rejection—the fear that their life doesn't matter in the eyes of others, that it's inconsequential, not measuring up. For most, this can transform into the fear of failure, a psychological death.

Life for many is about what they do and how successful they are in their accomplishments. They may wonder, "What do you think about what I do? How do you rate what I do? What if I fail at what I do? What would you think about me if I lost my job?"

This virus has destroyed many businesses and caused many to lose their jobs. Though no person is to blame for it, unemployment can lead to low self-esteem and even depression.

I recently spoke to a man who had slowly built a steady and lucrative consulting business. Forced to shut it down, he now faces the uncertainty of whether he'll ever reopen. Think of all the small business owners in this same predicament, dreading the same fate.

✶ Our Mortal Condition

Without a doubt, most people's greatest fear is death and dying.

Armand Nicholi, a clinical psychiatrist teaching at Harvard Medical School, believes that as we grow up, we begin to realize how temporal this life is and that it will someday come to an end.

> "This realization is extraordinarily painful. The unbelievable brevity of our lives conflicts with our deep-seated yearning for permanence and with our lifelong fear of being separated from those we love—a fear that haunts us from infancy to old age."

The brilliant French mathematician and philosopher Blaise Pascal believed most humans, deep down, are unhappy, and the reason is quite clear.

> "It is because of our mortal condition. Death is the most obvious fact of life. It slaps us in the face when we realize our own helplessness in overcoming it. Deep down we are haunted by the notion that, when we die, we experience the loss of everything in life."

In the midst of this pandemic, the greatest tragedy is the loss of human life. The elderly and those with underlying health issues recognize how this virus could be deadly to them. The fear of dying from the coronavirus hangs over the heads of many people, paralyzing their lives with fear.

The Modern Predicament

In the late 1940s, W. H. Auden wrote the famous poem,

"The Age of Anxiety." He created it during a time when sociologists, psychologists, and psychiatrists agreed that people were much more fearful and anxious than their parents' generation. Eighty years later, the problem is still not resolved. Our society is as anxious as ever, and the virus has only intensified the distress.

Dr. Tim Keller provides solid insight into the nature of our fear. He says we have drifted away from God as the source of a secure foundation. When we decide we don't need God, that we can live better without Him, on our own, autonomously, we throw open the door for fear to infiltrate our lives. When we move away from God, we experience a real sense of our finiteness here on earth, oftentimes inciting positions of the universe that are just too big to handle.

This reminds me of a story from my childhood. When I was six, I remember persuading my parents to let me go trick or treating with a few older boys on Halloween night. I was excited and having a blast until I realized I couldn't keep up with the group. Eventually, I became separated and had no clue where I was. As I wandered around by myself for what seemed like hours, I grew afraid and started to cry. It wasn't until I saw my dad in the distance that my tears turned to a smile, feeling safe in his presence. All fear had disappeared.

Clearly, I tried to take on something that was too big for me to handle. It's easy to believe we can run our lives better than God, but there is nothing more foolish than to think we have life under control when it is not controllable.

Chapter 1: Understanding Fear

A Key to Finding Peace

Do you know the moment a person experiences a true sense of peace in their lives? It's when they believe they are secure. A person finds security when he builds his life on that which can't be taken away. Conversely, insecurity is when you build your life on something that *can* be taken away. Note the key phrase: *build your life on.*

What is the foundation you have built your life upon? Is it something that you can lose? Can it be taken away from you?

Augustine believed your fears tell you a lot about yourself, that you can always follow your worries to that which you have built your life around.

The highly regarded existential psychologist, Rollo May, made this observation:

> *"Anxiety comes when something that you have put your real security in—something that made you feel in control, something that made you feel like you had an identity—is threatened or it implodes."*

Stephen Covey, in his insightful book, *The Seven Habits of Highly Effective People*, writes, "We all have a personal center, and whatever is at the center of your life is the source of your security."

Is there an absolute security, a true foundation that can always be relied upon? The Bible teaches that Christ should be that center.

One moral philosopher and writer, who undeniably grasped this concept, was C. S. Lewis. Notably one of 20th century's greatest thinkers, Lewis moved from atheism, to theism and, finally, to the Christian faith. In his search for truth, Lewis found it in the person of Jesus. He believed Christ was the one who could unify and guide his life, becoming his blessed and ultimate security.

CHAPTER 2

Preparing the Way

AT SOME point in our life's journey, we inevitably reach a clear and present understanding that no matter how hard we might try, we never find peace in ignorance or anxious concern. We cannot avoid our fears and expect to experience the rich promises of life. Instead, we must face the reality that there will be storms in our lives, prompting the question, "Will I be prepared?"

Dr. Paul Brand was a world-renowned hand surgeon, living and working among people afflicted with leprosy. Because of this, he spent most of his professional life studying human pain. After years of research, he concluded that the attitude we form prior to suffering and death determines how we are affected by it later.

In the 1990s, the Public Broadcasting System aired a serious and moving documentary, "Dying," directed and produced by Michael Roemer. In the film, Roemer spends

...me with people who are terminally ill with cancer during their last months of life. Having received permission from their families in advance, Roemer made a convincing observation at the conclusion of filming.

"People die in the way they have lived," he said. "Death becomes the expression of everything you are, and you can bring to it only what you have brought to life."

The documentary reveals that people who prepare for death discover their final days can be some of life's greatest moments.

The question to ponder is how do you prepare for pain, suffering and the storms of life? How do you prepare for death? Phillip Yancey offers insight.

"The best way to prepare for suffering is to work on a strong supportive life when you are healthy," he said. "You cannot suddenly fabricate foundations of strength. They must have been building all along, as you live your life."

The process starts by understanding how we are to walk through pain and suffering, and how to walk by faith. God gives us specific instruction in the Bible, serving as a powerful source of comfort and peace.

Tim Keller shares some powerful words on this in his compelling book, *Walking with God Through Pain and Suffering*.

> *"Once you are in a crisis, there is no time to sit down to give substantive study and attention to parts of the Bible. As a working pastor for nearly four decades, I have often sat beside people who were going through terrible troubles and silently wished they had taken the time to learn more about their faith before the tidal wave of*

> *trouble engulfed them. As we have seen, the main "reasons of the heart" that help us endure suffering are the foundational doctrines of the faith—creation and fall, atonement and resurrection. These are the profound and rich truths we need to grasp before we suffer, or we will be unprepared for it. And many of these lessons are very difficult to learn "on the job" when we are in the middle of adversity.*
>
> *A great deal of preparation for suffering is simple but crucial. It means developing a deep enough knowledge of the Bible and a strong and vital enough prayer life that you will neither be surprised by nor overthrown by affliction."*

Do we have the foundation that enables us to withstand the storms of life? If not, how do we prepare ourselves and how do we build that strong foundation to weather adversity and painful circumstances?

Jesus addresses this with an impressive message in the Sermon on the Mount:

> *"Therefore everyone who hears these words of mine and puts them into practice is like a wise man who built his house on the rock. The rain came down, the streams rose, and the winds blew and beat against that house; yet it did not fall, because it had its foundation on the rock. But everyone who hears these words of mine and does not put them into practice is like a foolish man who built his house on sand. The rain came down, the streams rose, and the winds blew and beat against that house and it fell with a great crash." (Mathew 7:24-27)*

Jesus is telling us in these verses that the storms in life are coming. It's just a matter of time. He also reveals that we can be prepared based on the foundation we build our lives upon.

If we are to build our lives on a foundation of solid rock, it is important to integrate Jesus's words and His truth into our lives. We must take the time to understand His teaching on how to respond to the storms of life. The central truths of the Bible can provide an encouraging foundation that enables us to find peace in the midst of hardship.

In the next chapter, we consider some of the foundational truths about God to help us better understand how to respond by faith.

CHAPTER 3

What We Need to Know About God

AS WE consider the storms of life, we need to seek to understand God and His perspective on pain and hardship. Many years ago, I heard this profound truth:

> *"In the midst of the storms of life, we either allow what we are experiencing to influence our view of God, or we allow our view of God to influence what we are experiencing."*

Too many people allow the painful circumstances of life to impact their view of God. It is easy to conclude He is an uncaring, harsh God. Many in our society abandon belief in Him because they deem a loving God would not allow bad things to happen to them.

However, if we seek to view and understand our painful circumstances from God's perspective and through the lens of Biblical truth, we will find them transformed. We will find God's peace.

Foundational Truths

In Psalm 50:21, we are told something interesting about the human perspective of God. In this verse God says, "You thought I was just like you." But He makes it clear He is not.

Without realizing, we presumptuously assume God is like us and that He should operate this world as we would, supporting our plans. How easy it can be to believe in God and get along with Him as long as He does what we want. However, if He deviates from what we want, it seems effortless to fire Him, as though He is an inept personal assistant, not doing His job. In Isaiah 55:8,9 God makes it quite clear:

> *"For My thoughts are not your thoughts, nor are your ways My ways declares the Lord. For as the heavens are higher than the earth, so My ways are higher than your ways, and My thoughts than your thoughts."*

We are being told by God, "I don't think like you. I don't see life as you see it. I don't see the storms of life as you see them. And I don't see this pandemic as you see it."

God's ways are much higher than ours, particularly as it relates to time. In II Peter 3:8, we are told that 1,000 years in our time is like a single day to God. If you do the math, 50 years of time on this earth is like an hour in His sight.

Chapter 3: What We Need to Know About God

God sees the big picture. We are not sure how long we will battle COVID-19, nor do we know the ultimate suffering that will come from it, but God sees far into the future, and His purposes in it will be revealed with the passage of time. We must recognize there is often a ripple effect that may take years for us to see.

Tim Keller shared a wondrous story in his book, *Walking With God Through Pain and Suffering*. Part of the story reflects his planting of the church, Redeemer Presbyterian, in New York City many years ago:

> "I sometimes ask people at my church in New York City, Redeemer Presbyterian, if they are glad the church exists. They are (thankfully!). Then I point out an interesting string of 'coincidences' that brought it all about. Redeemer exists to a great degree because my wife, Kathy, and I were sent to New York City to start this as a new church. Why were we sent? It was because we joined a Presbyterian denomination that encouraged church planting and that sent us out. But why did we join a Presbyterian denomination? We joined it because in the very last semester of my last year at seminary, I had two courses under a particular professor who convinced me to adopt the doctrines and beliefs of Presbyterianism. But why was that professor at the seminary at that time? He was there only because, after a long period of waiting, he was finally able to get his visa as a citizen of Great Britain to come and teach in the United States.
>
> This professor had been hired by my U.S. seminary but had been having a great deal of trouble getting a visa. For

> *various reasons at the time the process was very clogged and there was an enormous backlog of applications. What was it that broke through all the red tape so he could get his visa and come in time to teach me that last semester? I was told that his visa process was facilitated because one of the students at our seminary at the time was able to give the school administration an unusually high-level form of help. The student was the son of the sitting president of the United States at the time. Why was his father president? It was because the former president, Richard Nixon, had to resign as a result of the Watergate scandal. But why did the Watergate scandal even occur? I understand that it was because a night watchman noticed an unlatched door.*
>
> *What if the security guard had not noticed that door? In that case – nothing else in that long string of 'coincidences' would have ever occurred. And there would be no Redeemer Presbyterian Church in the city. Do you think all that happened by accident? I don't. If that did not all happen by accident, nothing happens by accident. I like to say to people at Redeemer: If you are glad for this church, then Watergate happened for you."*

Recalling the above story, I'm reminded that Charles Colson, a member of Richard Nixon's cabinet, went to prison over his involvement with Watergate. In the process, he became a Christian. After serving his sentence, he founded Prison Fellowship, which is one of the largest prison ministries in the world, touching hundreds of thousands of lives.

Watergate took place more than 50 years ago and was an extremely dark period in our nation's history. Rarely do we get a glimpse of how God redeems the painful storms of life. Years from now, I believe we will see how God has used this virus for a great purpose.

Five Significant Truths

Ask yourself, "What do I need to know about God that will enable me to properly interpret the pain I experience?"

I contend there are five significant truths that transform if not the storms themselves, but how we weather them. We must embrace these truths if we are to walk through storms with peace and confidence.

Truth #1: We are of great value

In Matthew 6:25, Jesus tells us not to worry about our lives and circumstances. Then in verse 26, He tells us why.

> *"Look at the birds in the air, they do not sow or reap or gather into barns, and yet your heavenly Father feeds them. Are you not worth much more than they?"*

This verse reveals that we are of great value to God. In Jeremiah 31:3, He shares that He loves us with an everlasting love. But it is more than God's love for His creation. As Christians we are adopted into God's family. He loves us as a father loves his own child. However, God tells us His love for us is so much greater than our love for our own children. As sinful people, our love for our children is flawed. God's love for us is a perfect love.

Therefore, first and foremost we must know that in the midst of our pain, He has not abandoned us, He values us as a father values and loves his own children.

Truth #2: God is sovereign

Jesus tells us in Matthew 10:29, "Are not two sparrows sold for a cent? Yet, not one of them will fall to the ground without your father's consent and notice."

In other words, God is sovereign over all of life. If there is a storm in your life, He has allowed it to come into your life. It can only come into our lives by His consent.

Truth #3: Nothing is too difficult for Him

In Jeremiah 32:27, we are told, "Behold, I am the Lord, the God of all flesh, is anything too difficult for me?"

God is capable of removing any storm from our lives whenever He chooses. However, if it remains in your life and continues to be there, it is surely there for a reason. Maybe there is purpose in it.

Truth #4: God is with you

The Apostle Paul was an incredibly bold man as he fearlessly moved into hostile regions proclaiming the Gospel message to people who opposed him. He was in jail often and beaten a number of times. You would think Paul had no fear.

However, in Acts 18:9,10 Paul was in Corinth and God says to him, "Do not be afraid any longer, but go on speaking and do not be silent, for I am with you." He goes on to say that he will not be harmed.

This reveals a very important truth that we all need to grasp and believe. We are told throughout scripture that if you are one of His children, God is with you. He seems to remind us of this when we are afraid. We are told:

- **Isaiah 41:10:** "Do not fear, for I am with you; Do not anxiously look about you, for I am your God. I will strengthen you, surely I will help you, surely I will uphold you with My righteous right hand."
- **Deuteronomy 31:6:** "Be strong and courageous, do not be afraid or tremble at them, for the LORD your God is the one who goes with you. He will not fail you or forsake you."
- **Deuteronomy 31:8:** "The LORD is the one who goes ahead of you; He will be with you. He will not fail you or forsake you. Do not fear or be dismayed."

Then David tells us in Psalm 23 that even when we walk through the valley of the shadow of death, He will be with us.

This appears to be a highly crucial truth to reflect on in times of stress and fear—God is with us. Because of this, we have nothing to fear.

Truth #5: Hardship is used for good

Lastly, we are told in Romans 8:28, "God is causing all things to work together for good to those who love Him and are called according to His purpose."

When I first read this verse, it offered tremendous encouragement, particularly when I realized life was full of difficulty. The dilemma for me was how to interpret the meaning of "good."

I have always been intrigued by the word "good" as it relates to our lives. From God's perspective, what is our ultimate good? Psalm 73 reveals that being close to God is very good. The Psalmist says, "the nearness of God is my good." It seems logical that, in going through a storm, it is much easier for us to trust God when we are close to Him.

God uses the storms of life to draw us into a closer relationship with Him, which leads to our well-being.

However, as I was thinking about Romans 8:28 and digging further into the text, I soon realized the significance of the next verse in Romans. What I considered to be the good life was not at all what God had revealed it to be. In Romans 8:29, we learn the ultimate good in life is that we be conformed to the image of His son.

This was the exact moment it finally dawned on me that God's desire for me and for all people is to become more like Jesus—increasingly like Jesus. Up until that time, my entire life had focused on what I was achieving and experiencing. God, on the other hand, was more concerned with the type of man I was becoming.

However, as a man, I realized I live in a culture where men do not believe that "Christlikeness" is manly or masculine. Often, men consider that to be like Christ is to be religious, withdrawing from the world.

As I studied Jesus' life, I realized Jesus was not religious—at least, not the way we typically think of as being religious. He lived in a highly religious culture, one where many of the religious people found Him to be contemptible.

He did not follow their traditions to the letter of the Law. Many of the religious leaders did not like the people He hung out with. He spoke harshly to the Pharisees and other men of high status and teaching. He made political matters worse, as many of their followers began to follow Him and His teachings. What I now realize is this: Christ-likeness is no way what I thought it to be. In essence, it is:

- To be transformed in our character
- To grow in wisdom
- To love and have compassion
- To build high-quality relationships

Also, as a man, I understand that character, wisdom and love make up the essence of what it means to be an authentic man.

So, I ask you, what is the great good in your life? If it is comfort, prosperity and pleasure, then the storms of life are nothing more than a calamity, which should be avoided at all costs.

However, if the ultimate good in life is to become like Christ, then you will see that God uses the storms of life to bring that to pass. And, therefore, you will see hardship as a blessing—a gift for your ultimate good.

CHAPTER 4

Does God Use Suffering Purposefully?

DR. PAUL BRAND, the famous orthopedic surgeon quoted earlier, spent the first 25 years of his life in London. He served his medical internship there during the most harrowing days and nights of The Blitz, as the German Luftwaffe continued to pound a proud city into rubble. With the bombing campaign in full force, Brand remained steadfast.

> "Physical hardship was a constant companion, the focal point of nearly every conversation and front-page headline," Brand said. "Yet I have never lived among people so buoyant; now I read that 60 percent of Londoners who lived through the Blitz remember it as the happiest period of their lives."

You have to wonder how this frightening experience could be one of the happiest times in your life. Brand says they "suffered gladly for a cause." There was purpose in their suffering, defending their beloved country against an evil tyrant who wanted to destroy them.

Dr. Henry K. Beecher of Harvard Medical School made an interesting observation among the 215 wounded men from the Anzio beachhead during World War II:

> *"Only one in four soldiers with serious injuries (fractures, amputations, penetrated chests or cerebrums) asked for morphine, though it was freely available. They simply did not need help with the pain, and indeed many of them denied feeling pain at all. Beecher, an anesthesiologist, contrasted the soldiers' reactions to what he had seen in private practice where 80 percent of patients recovering from surgical wounds begged for morphine or other narcotics.*
>
> *Here you have two groups of people suffering from the same exact injuries. The soldiers' responses to pain were impacted by the fact that their injuries carried with them a sense of meaning – a result of being involved in a significant mission for their country. They also had a sense of gratitude that they had survived. Yet, the civilian patients with the same exact wounds saw their injuries as being depressing and calamitous, and thus 'they begged for morphine or other narcotics.'"*

Just before Jesus was taken into custody, He made this point to His disciples in John 16:21:

> *"Whenever a woman is in labor, she has pain because her hour has come; but, when she gives birth to the*

child, she no longer remembers the anguish because of the joy that a child has been born into the world." (author paraphrase)

A woman's pain produces something with great meaning—she has helped create a new life, and for that reason, she can contemplate repeating the experience without fear and worry. The point that I am making is crucial to grasp. It is foundational if you are going to deal effectively with painful circumstances.

I recently studied how God uses pain and suffering purposefully in our lives. This is something we normally don't consider when going through the storms of life. Here are my findings:

First purpose

Think about how adversity strengthens us, making us more resilient. It helps us realize we can make it through future storms with less anxiety.

Recently, I had a thoughtful conversation with a man who owns a large company. During the Great Recession in 2009-2010, his company was on the verge of bankruptcy; the banks were calling all of his loans. He barely survived. But, when talking to him recently, I asked him how God used that time in his life.

First, he said he learned a financial lesson. Over the last ten years, he has diligently worked to get his company out of debt. Today his company is debt-free and the stress from the current recession isn't near as intense. He also knows he has the resilience to make it through this difficult economic time created by the coronavirus. He's been there before.

James provides an interesting reflection on this:

> *"Consider it all joy, my brethren, when you encounter various trials, knowing that the testing of your faith produces endurance, and let endurance have its perfect result, so that you might be spiritually mature and complete, lacking in nothing."* (James 1:2-4)

This is so counterintuitive. Why would James tell us to be joyful when trials enter into our lives? He is saying that you can count on it that God is using it purposefully in your life. So be joyful!

Second purpose

It's important for us to realize how the storms of life can humble us. It can transform our attitudes toward ourselves and remove unrealistic self-regard and pride we may possess. What I've witnessed is how this pandemic is causing a lot of men to realize they are not bulletproof and are clearly not in control of the circumstances that surround them.

In II Corinthians 12:7-10, the Apostle Paul speaks of a painful thorn in his flesh that God has allowed. Paul says twice that the thorn is being used by God to "keep me from exalting myself." In other words, there is purpose in it.

Third purpose

The storms of life can often change your priorities and

your goals. Tim Keller says suffering tends to force us out of certain life agendas and into others. He says suffering will profoundly change your relationship with things that are too important to you.

We fail to realize that sometimes fear results from the misplaced affections of our hearts. Particularly when these affections are threatened. Augustine said that most people's main problem, that which brings so much trouble and fear into their lives, is their hearts are filled with disordered loves.

Tim Keller said it best:

"If anyone but God is the main love of your hearts, you will be a fool. You will make poor choices and your priorities will be out of order. In the process, you are inviting all types of stress, fear and worry into your life."

I don't think we realize how so much of the worry and fear in our lives would be eliminated if Christ was our first love, our first priority and the foundation of our lives. When that is the case, we won't be so attached to the temporal things of life, which will cause our fears to diminish.

Fourth purpose

Suffering can strengthen our relationship with God as nothing else can. It drives people to God in ways that never happen when all is going well. As Oswald Chambers put it:

> *"The great difficulty spiritually is to concentrate on God, and it is His blessings that make it difficult. Troubles nearly always make us look to God; His blessings are apt to make us look elsewhere."*

Furthermore, God often uses pain in the lives of non-Christians to draw them to Himself. C. S. Lewis says God uses pain as a megaphone to rouse a deaf world. He acknowledges that pain as a megaphone is a terrible instrument and causes some people to turn away from God. However, Lewis believed it gave certain people the only opportunity to repent. In Lewis' own words, "Pain removes the veil; it plants the flag of truth within the fortress of a rebel soul."

This is what happened in the life of the Russian Nobel Prize winning author Aleksandr Solzhenitsyn. In his 20s he was thrown into prison after making some critical remarks about Joseph Stalin. He entered prison as an atheist, but at some point, had a powerful conversion experience and became a Christian. He concluded that God used severe hardship to make a spiritual breakthrough in his life. He saw how purposeful going to prison was in his life. As he walked out of prison after serving an eight-year sentence, he uttered these powerful words:

> *"I bless you, prison. I bless you for being in my life. For there, lying on the rotting prison straw, I learned the object of life is not prosperity as I had grown up believing, but the maturing of the soul."*

Chapter 4: Does God Use Suffering Purposefully?

How could anyone consider eight years in prison a blessing? Eight years separated from one's family and friends. Solzhenitsyn realized God had made a spiritual breakthrough in his life through prison. A breakthrough that otherwise might never have happened.

CHAPTER 5

Responding to the Storms of Life

THE MOST important truth you can learn about the storms of life is how to respond to them once they blow into your world. As a Christian, you can respond in a godly way or a godless way. Godlessness is to exclude God from places where He belongs. It is to put Him on the sidelines. In this chapter, I help provide an understanding of how to respond to hardships in a godly way, because our response is everything.

Many of life's most sacred truths can be learned only as we walk through our individual storms. We all experience them. Yet, all we ever seem to want is relief and comfort from the challenges they can present. We demand instant solutions, but what we fail to recognize is that although God can solve each of our problems, instant solutions are not important to Him. How we respond to our struggles is what He finds important.

I find that people can instinctively respond to their negative circumstances not only with fear, but also with anger and bitterness. "Why me?" they ask. "This is not fair. I don't deserve this!"

Caught up in the process of cursing the realities of life, we most often discover the pain actually continues to increase.

Phillip Yancey wrote about the highly influential 20th century Swiss psychologist Paul Tournier's insight in the book *Where Is God When It Hurts?* "Only rarely are we the masters of events, but [along with those who help us] we are responsible for our reactions." In other words, we are accountable for the way we respond to the struggles we encounter. Tournier believed that a positive, active, creative response to a life challenge develops us, while a negative, angry one only debilitates us, stunting our growth. Tournier also believed the right response at the right moment might actually determine the course of a person's entire life. He found that humans are often presented with rare opportunities to develop and grow only through hardship and trial. "That, in fact, was why he [Tournier] moved away from the traditional pattern of diagnosis and treatment and began to address his patients' emotional and spiritual needs as well," Yancy said.

Looking at it from another perspective, Charles Swindoll provides his take on life.

> *"I am convinced that life is 10% what happens to me and 90% how I react to it."*

So, how do we respond in a Godly manner, how do we

respond in a way that pleases God? How do we walk by faith?

Responding by Faith

In Psalm 121:1, we are told, "I lift up my eyes to the mountains, for where shall my help come?" My help comes from the Lord, who made heaven and earth." God is referred to by His people throughout Scripture as their "help" or "helper."

In John 14, Jesus refers to the Holy Spirit as the helper. God is telling us, *I am your helper, will you let me help you?*

When a storm enters our lives, either we lift our eyes to God, bringing our fears into His venue, or we gaze at our circumstances from a godless perspective, letting fear run wild in our imagination. The latter results in an emotional downward spiral.

Reflecting on this, consider these two verses. Hebrews 4:16 is especially significant. We are told, "Therefore let us draw near with confidence to the throne of grace, so that we may receive mercy and find grace to help in time of need."

We are to approach God and His throne of grace. For this is where we find grace to help us in time of need. Grace is God's divine enablement, His strength and power. As someone once told me, grace is when God enables me to do that which I can't do myself. And the scripture is clear in James 4:6: "God gives His grace only to the humble."

We must approach Him with humility and pray, "Father, I am struggling with the circumstances I find myself in, I am fearful and anxious. I cannot deliver myself and

I look to you to give me the grace to find strength and peace. I thank you for hearing my prayer. I pray this in Christ's name, Amen."

A second powerful verse is from Isaiah 26:3: "The steadfast of mind You will keep in perfect peace, because he trusts in You." The key word in this passage is "steadfast." Steadfast means "firmly fixed in place, immovable." So, our minds need to be firmly fixed in place on God. It needs to be focused on what He has told us and what we know to be true of Him, particularly as it relates to the storms of life. (See Chapter 2.)

Remember, fear begins in the mind; it then runs wild in the imagination. This is why the struggles today in people's lives are mental. As healthcare professionals put it, "We have a mental health crisis because of this pandemic."

In the chapters that follow, we will consider how we as Christians are to respond in a godly way to the pain and suffering of life.

CHAPTER 6

A Grateful Heart

THINK BACK to Chapter Four where we considered the question, "Does God use suffering purposefully?" We looked at the life of Aleksandr Solzenitsyn, who upon getting out of prison after eight hard years, uttered the words, "I bless you prison, I bless you for being in my life." Solzenitsyn saw how God had used his suffering in prison to humble him and bring him to faith in Christ. He was actually saying, "I thank you prison for being in my life." He saw its purpose and was incredibly grateful for it.

This is critical to recognize as an important part of responding faithfully to the storms of life. It is counterintuitive, as was James words when he wrote: "Consider it all joy when you encounter various trials." James knew trials would be used by God to develop us spiritually, and that we should respond joyfully. Paul, on the other hand, says we should give thanks.

Among the first pioneers to discover the impact emotions play in a person's health was Austrian-Canadian scientist Dr. Hans Selye (1907-1982). On his quest to better understand stress and human emotion, he wrote a total of 30 books in his endeavor. Toward the end of his life, Dr. Selye summarized his research, declaring that anger, bitterness and revenge are the emotions most harmful to our health and well-being. He also concluded that a heart of gratitude is the single most nourishing response that leads to good health. Gratitude and thanksgiving are like therapy for the soul.

Selye recognized, if you don't have a grateful heart, you will grow bitter.

So, how does thanksgiving play a role in our response to trials and difficulty? The Apostle Paul says in Philippians 4:6,7:

> *"Do not be anxious about anything, but in every situation, by prayer and petition, with thanksgiving, present your requests to God. And the peace of God, which transcends all understanding, will guard your hearts and your minds in Christ Jesus."*

And then in I Thessalonians 5:18:

> *"Give thanks in all circumstances; for this is God's will for you in Christ Jesus."*

When you are in the midst of a storm and you have no idea how it's going to turn out nor how God is going to use it for good in your life, thanksgiving places confidence in God and the ultimate outcome. It is an act of faith, as you are trusting Him with the outcome and are confident He is going to use it for good in your life. Paul tells us in Philippians that this is essential in experiencing God's peace.

Consider approaching Him with this perspective and this prayer:

> *"Lord, I don't know what you are doing in my life or why you have allowed this, but I thank you for how you are going to use this purposefully in my life."*

> *"I pray that what I am experiencing will lead to spiritual growth, inner transformation and a deeper relationship with You. And I thank you that You will bring this to pass."*

This is what it means to walk by faith, trusting Him with your circumstances and the ultimate outcome. When you do this, God begins to move in your life by giving you strength and peace. He also might choose to move in the circumstances that are causing fear and pain.

Please know God loves it when we, His children, trust Him and walk by faith. We are told in Hebrews 11:6, "without faith, it is impossible for us to please Him."

CHAPTER 7

Acceptance

ORTHOPEDIC surgeon Paul Brand, mentioned in Chapter Three, lived in London for 25 years, spending a portion of that time living through The Blitz. After the war ended and he finished his internship, he moved to India where he lived for 27 years. It was there that he began to treat leprosy patients. Although India was a land of poverty and omnipresent suffering, Brand was amazed how the people bore suffering with dignity and calm acceptance.

The kind of acceptance displayed by the people of India is absolutely necessary for us to follow if we are to respond to the storms of life in a godly way.

Think of Jesus in the garden of Gethsemane just before he was arrested. He wandered a short distance by Himself and prayed, "My Father, if it is possible, let this cup pass from Me, yet not as I will, but as You will." (Matthew 26:39) This is an appropriate prayer for any of us, recognizing we want God's will done in our lives regardless of the circumstances.

Hours later after Jesus prayed, Roman soldiers approached to apprehend Him. At that moment, Peter drew a sword and cut off the ear of the servant of the high priest. Jesus looked at Peter and asked, "… the cup which my Father has given Me, shall I not drink it?" (John 18:11)

God the Father had made it clear that He must drink the cup of the cross; it was absolutely necessary. Jesus calmly accepted it, for God's will had to be done.

Probably the best example of acceptance is found in Mary's life. She was a young woman engaged to be married to Joseph, a local carpenter who lived there in Nazareth. Before they were married, Mary was visited by the angel Gabriel. He tells her she has found favor with God and "will conceive in her womb and bear a son and you shall name Him Jesus." She, of course, responds as you would expect, "How can this be, I am a virgin?" (Luke 1:26-34) Gabriel then explains that the Holy Spirit would come upon her and she would be impregnated.

Here she is, soon to be married to Joseph, and is told she is to become pregnant, and that Joseph would not be the father. These are brutal circumstances to find yourself in as a young, unmarried woman in this highly strict Jewish culture.

However, Mary's response to the angel is powerful. She doesn't argue, nor does she panic. She calmly accepts what she's been told, responding, "I am the Lord's servant, may it be done to me as you have said." (Luke 1:38) Mary humbly accepted this, exhibiting real trust.

When a storm enters your life, consider approaching the Lord with this prayer:

> *"Lord, I am not sure what you are seeking to accomplish, but I am your servant, let this play out in my life according to Your will."*

This is faith. This is a declaration to God that "I trust You."

When Your Picture Blows Up

Nearly five years ago, I attended a seminar on the importance of acceptance and it was one of the best teachings I've ever heard on the topic. Julie Sparkman, a counselor, speaker and author, taught the seminar.

She said that whether we are aware of it or not, we all have a picture of how we want life to be. Your picture involves people in your life and your circumstances. When these are closely aligned, life is good. Everything is going the way you want it to go.

However, when there is a gap between your picture and reality, or if your picture just blows up, it brings pressure, stress, pain and fear into your life.

Think of how many of these life pictures have blown up because of this pandemic. Large weddings have been cancelled. A close friend's father died, with the family unable to honor him at a public funeral. Think of how devasted athletes are with cancelled sports. Graduations have been cancelled or postponed. Then you have the record-breaking job losses and businesses being closed for good. And then there's all of the sickness and deaths. Our response is critical.

It's important to know there is nothing wrong with having a picture, wanting life to turn out a certain way. It's natural to hope for things, as it is a part of our hardwiring.

However, one of the reasons we experience pain and distress when our picture explodes is because it's too important to us. Our picture becomes the source of joy and peace in our lives. When it doesn't become a reality, life becomes destitute and we experience despair.

When this happens, we commit what the Bible calls "idolatry." What is interesting is that idols are not sinful things. They are generally good things, gifts from God, that we have elevated to ultimate things. Or as Phillip Yancey said, "We take something good and grant to it a power in our lives it was never meant to have."

When our picture becomes an idol and blows up, the pain and stress are amplified because we believe we will never be happy without our picture.

Recognize this; the picture is not the problem. We are the problem. As I mentioned in Chapter Four, quoting Augustine, our hearts are filled with disordered loves—idolatry. We are definitively convinced that our pictures are necessary for our ultimate well-being.

So, what do we do?

Accepting God's Yoke

Jesus gives us sound instructions for this in Matthew 11:28-30:

Chapter 7: Acceptance

*"Come to Me, all who are weary and heavy-laden, and I will give you rest. Take My yoke upon you and learn from Me, for I am gentle and humble in heart, and **you will find rest for your souls**. For My yoke is easy and My burden is light."*

Jesus is telling us to surrender our yoke to Him, and then take His yoke. Applying this teaching to our picture, Jesus is saying surrender your picture to Me and take My picture. Accept the picture I have for you.

One could ask, "Why?" Because God is in control. As we look at our shattered pictures, He tells us that He is not absent. He is in our circumstances, saying, "I am with you." Furthermore, as a Christian, He is in me. His Holy Spirit resides in me.

When we talk about surrendering our picture and taking His, isn't that what Mary did? She clearly had a picture of her future. Mary was going to be a wife to Joseph, who the Bible tells us was a good man and gainfully employed as a carpenter. I am sure her picture not only included marriage to Joseph, but also a family, a home, a life together. Out of the blue, Gabriel comes along and blows up her picture. Mary, of course, surrenders her vision, taking God's picture for her own, having no idea where it would lead.

We are going to find ourselves during this pandemic and over the course of our lives in circumstances where our pictures blow up. When this happens, will we respond in a godly manner, giving up our picture to accept His?

Going back to Jesus' words in Matthew 11, we must understand the purpose of a yoke back in Biblical times.

It provided the means of harnessing the effort of two animals to accomplish a common objective. It is crucial during times when your picture and reality are not in alignment that we embrace God's yoke. Although it's a natural reaction for us to beg Him to give us our picture, we should embrace God's yoke, God's objective in our circumstance.

Our prayer should be, "Lord, I am committed to You and Your objective for my life. I am with You in whatever You are trying to accomplish in me."

My Other Role

"Learn from me." That's exactly what Jesus tells us in Matthew 11:29. He desires to lead and teach us. Julie Sparkmon believes we should ask God, "What is my role in this, what would You have me do?"

In I Samuel 29, David is about to become King, while still being pursued by Saul. Finding favor with the Philistine king, David, his men and their families are given place to live—a town called Ziglag.

Later, David and his men are away, negotiating with the Philistines. When they return to Ziglag, they learn the Amalekites have come, captured their wives, children and possessions, and burned the town.

As it turns out, none of their wives or children are killed, but David and his men don't initially know this. Finding their town destroyed, David and his men "lifted their voices and wept until there was no strength in them to weep."

In Samuel 30:6, we learn that David is greatly distressed not only because his family has been taken, but because his men are considering stoning him, blaming him for all that has happened.

Though David is greatly distressed and full of fear, we never see him panic or make an impetuous decision. His response to these stressful circumstances is a powerful lesson for us all.

We are told he first "strengthens himself in the Lord." He looks to God and focuses on what is true of God with a steadfast mind. And then he asks God what he should do. He does not impetuously react to what has happened. With great poise, he waits on God's instructions and leading.

This is what we are called to do in the storms of life. First, to look to God to find peace and strength. Then, to seek to understand our role and what He would have us do.

God tells David to pursue the Amalekites, which he does. They recapture their families and their possessions. Let us remember David's response as our example.

A Story of Acceptance

Forty years ago, I read a book with a story in it I've never forgotten. The book, *A Man Called Peter*, was a bestselling biography back in the early 1960s, sharing the life of Peter Marshall and written by his wife Catherine. Peter was a highly regarded pastor in Washington D.C. as well as the chaplain of the United States Senate for many years.

During Peter and Catherine's marriage, Catherine contracted tuberculosis, eventually becoming an invalid. Praying to God, she believed He would heal her. Many days of prayer passed with no change in her condition.

Catherine became angry and discouraged. Yet, after reading a story of the life of a missionary, she realized how poorly she was responding to her circumstances:

> "I had been demanding of God. I had claimed health as my right. Furthermore, I had never, for one moment, stopped rebelling against tuberculosis or against the invalidism it had induced. I had not faced reality. The right way, then, must be the only way left—that of submission and surrender to the situation as it was. (This was acceptance.)
>
> "Privately, with tears eloquent of the reality of what I was doing, I lay in bed and prayed, 'Lord, I've done everything I've known how to do, and it hasn't been good enough. I'm desperately weary of the struggle of trying to persuade You to give me what I want. I'm beaten, whipped, through. If You want me to be an invalid for the rest of my life, all right. Here I am. Do anything You like with me and my life.'"

When Catherine said this prayer to God, she was at her parents' home without Peter. She was preparing to go to bed, and as she was dozing off, she thought to herself, "There was no trace of graciousness about the gift of my life and will, nothing victorious, nothing expectant. I had no faith left, as I understood faith. Nevertheless, a strange deep peace settled into my heart."

At 3 a.m., she was awakened from her sleep, experiencing a real and powerful presence of Jesus. She referred to it as "an intensity of power."

From that day forward, she began to slowly heal, never with any retrogression. Several months later, the doctor pronounced she was completely healed.

What an exemplary example of what it looks like to surrender your picture and accept what God has for you.

We experience God's peace and His power when we accept what He is doing in our lives. It is truly a powerful way to respond to the storms of life because this is an act of faith, and God always responds to faith.

CHAPTER 8

One Day at a Time

I N THE middle of the Sermon on the Mount, found in Matthew 6:25-34, Jesus addresses fear and anxiety. He points to a real concern of meeting basic needs that caused worry for people in Biblical times. Jesus says to them:

> *"For this reason, I say to you, do not be anxious for your life, as to what you shall eat, or what you shall drink; nor for your body, as to what you shall put on. Is not life more than food, and the body than clothing?*
>
> *Look at the birds of the air, that they do not sow, neither do they reap, nor gather into barns, and yet your heavenly Father feeds them. Are you not worth much more than they?*
>
> *And which of you by being anxious can add a single cubit to his life's span?*

And why are you anxious about clothing? Observe how the lilies of the field grow; they do not toil nor do they spin, yet I say to you that even Solomon in all his glory did not clothe himself like one of these.

But if God so arrays the grass of the field, which is alive today and tomorrow is thrown into the furnace, will He not much more do so for you, O men of little faith?"

Do not worry then, saying, 'What will we eat?' or 'What will we drink?' or 'What will we wear for clothing?'

For the Gentiles eagerly seek all these things; for your heavenly Father knows that you need all these things.

But seek first His kingdom and His righteousness, and all these things will be added to you.

So do not worry about tomorrow; for tomorrow will care for itself. Each day has enough trouble of its own.

In today's age of plenty, at least in America, not everyone worries if they'll have food to eat or clothes to wear. Yet, this pandemic has caused us to question the possibility of shortages in areas considered to be "the necessities of life."

There's been ample footage of press covering possible meat shortages due to meat-packing plants shutting down after hundreds of employees contracted the virus.

In the pandemic's first week of nonessential businesses closings, my wife asked me to stop by Target for toilet paper. When I got to the paper product aisle, I was shocked to see empty shelves. A complete wipeout of toilet paper—even paper towels and tissues.

Jesus tells us not to worry about our basic needs being met. He cares for us. Just as He cares for the birds in the sky, He will meet our needs because we are of such extraordinary value to Him.

Jesus then shares an important teaching about our fears in verse 34, saying, "So do not worry about tomorrow, for tomorrow will care for itself. Each day has enough trouble of its own."

Jesus is contrasting tomorrow versus today. The future and the present. Worry and fear are clearly about tomorrow and the uncertainty over what is going to happen tomorrow.

Author and scholar David Wells wrote the following passage on fear and modern life. He says:

> *"The world intrudes upon us as it never has before. One of the surest indications of this is that the levels of anxiety have never been higher. And why are we more anxious? There are no doubt many reasons, including a heightened tempo in the workplace, greater economic insecurity, too many choices, and perhaps family breakdown. What is more, the extraordinary rapidity of change in our society powerfully fixes our attention on the future, for we need to anticipate events*

that are in the making in order to avoid what will be harmful and to capitalize on what will be beneficial. Anxiety, however, is nothing more than living out the future before it arrives, and modernity obliges us to do this many times over. The future is thereby greatly intensified for us."

Jesus provides us with wise guidance as He stresses the importance of living in the present, focused on the day in front of us. As we are encouraged by the Psalmist, "This is the day that the Lord has made, let us rejoice and be glad in this day." (Psalm 118:24) Not tomorrow.

Living in the Joy of the Moment

For many years I had a wonderful relationship with my ophthalmologist Jim Collier. He was a strong, godly man, and to my good fortune, we struck up a friendship. I remember receiving the sad news that Jim had cancer. Though not a smoker, the cancer was in his lungs.

Six months before he died, he invited me to join him for lunch. I went to his home, and we sat at his kitchen table, eating sandwiches. It was an incredible experience for me. I was amazed at how calm and tranquil he was, totally at peace.

Jim told me he knew his prognosis wasn't a good one. Then he mentioned something I've never forgotten.

"God has given me the grace to live in the joy of the moment," he said.

Live in the present. He knew that if he focused on the future, he'd experience despair. God enabled him to live in the present, as Jesus instructs us to do.

I realized there was nothing more he desired than to have more time to spend with his wife, his children and grandchildren. But then he told me:

"I would not trade what I am experiencing for anything," I was at a loss for words. He was referring to experiencing the presence of God in his life as he faced this deadly disease.

As I look back upon that day, I suggest an important application. When we are weighed down over the uncertainty over what is going to happen tomorrow, humbly go before Christ and ask Him,

> *"Lord, I pray that you will give me the grace to live one day at a time. That I might live in the present as You have instructed me. I realize I can't do this on my own, so I look to You to enable me to do that which I cannot do myself."*

I believe this is how Jim faced his circumstances, allowing him to live out the balance of his days in peace, one day at a time, in the joy of the moment.

CHAPTER 9

Experiencing God's Peace

JUST BEFORE Jesus is crucified, He shares important truths with his disciples about experiencing peace. He tells them He is preparing to leave and that where He is going, they cannot follow. It shakens them, but He then seeks to give them words of comfort.

In John 14:27, he says, "Peace I leave with you; My peace I give to you, not as the world gives do I give you. Do not let your heart be troubled, nor let it be fearful."

Notice that He doesn't just say "peace," He instead says "My peace" so that your hearts will not be troubled or fearful. This is significant.

In II Thessalonians 3:16, Paul says God wants to grant us peace in every circumstance we face. It is His peace.

In Romans 15:13, Paul speaks specifically how He wants to give us that peace. He says, "Now may the God of hope fill you with all joy and peace in believing, so that you will abound in hope by the power of the Holy Spirit." The Holy Spirit is the way in which we experience God's peace.

When a person by faith surrenders his or her life to Christ, the Holy Spirit resides in that person's life. In Ephesians 1:13, Paul refers to it as a "sealing" of the Holy Spirit. In Galatians 4:6, Paul says, "God has sent forth the Spirit of His Son into our hearts …" Then in Colossians 1:27, he speaks of "Christ in you," who is living in you through the Holy Spirit.

As you read through the New Testament, after Pentecost when God unleashes the Holy Spirit, there appears to be a difference in the Spirit coming into your life at salvation (where it is sealed in you,) and then experiencing the power of the Holy Spirit.

In many sections of the book of Acts, the phrase "filled with the Holy Spirit" or "walking in the Spirit" surfaces. In Acts 13:52, it is referred to as a daily continuous flowing of the Spirit into our lives.

We are given two metaphors to help us understand the flowing of the Holy Spirit. In John chapter 15, Jesus explains to the disciples that since He is leaving them, they will be functioning spiritually in a new way. He provides an illustration of a vine and a branch. The key visual to the illustration is the sap flowing from the vine into the branch so it can bear fruit. This is a picture of the Holy Spirit flowing from the vine into us, the branch.

Another metaphor is of water flowing. In John 7:37-39, Jesus gives us an explanation of the Spirit flowing into us by making reference to rivers of living water. This is what Jesus actually says:

> "Now on the last day, the great day of the feast, Jesus stood and cried out, saying, 'If any man is thirsty, let him come to Me and drink.
>
> He who believes in Me, as the Scripture said, 'From his innermost being shall flow rivers of living water.'
>
> But this He spoke of the Spirit, whom those who believed in Him were to receive; for the Spirit was not yet given, because Jesus was not yet glorified."

The Amplified version of the Bible says, "the rivers of living water will flow continuously."

The person who shared the significance of these three verses with me is my good friend and mentor John Riddle:

> "Before we talk about the passage, we need to understand the context in which it occurred. The people were celebrating the Feast of the Tabernacles which was held annually to remember God's supernatural provision for Israel during the forty years in the wilderness when manna and water were provided, clothes did not wear out, etc. The purpose of the feast was to express appreciation to God for survival of the nation during those years. On the last day of the feast, all males within 90 miles of Jerusalem were required to appear at the temple. The high priest poured out water from a pitcher, reminding the people of the promise in Joel 2:28, 29 where God promised to pour out His Spirit so that the people would serve Him in power."

The scripture in Joel that he refers to is quoted by Peter at Pentecost. In Acts 2:17, Peter says, "And it shall be in the last days that I will pour forth my spirit on all mankind." Joel spoke these words in the ninth century B.C., predicting that at some point in the future, God would make the outpouring of His Spirit available to all mankind.

There are those who think that the thrust of these words is evangelical, teaching the need for Christ to satisfy the thirst of the soul. But, in the context of when it was given, "the last day of the feast," Jesus was referring to the prophet Joel's words that says one day in the future, "I will pour out My Spirit on My people" so that they might serve Me with power.

Being Filled

Paul makes a compelling observation on walking in the power of the Holy Spirit in Ephesians 5:18. He says, "And do not get drunk with wine but be filled with the Spirit." Dr. Lewis Sperry Chafer, a great theologian and the first president of Dallas Theological Seminary, also reflects on this passage from Ephesians:

> *"Being filled with the Spirit is compared to intoxication in which wine affects the entire person, both the mental activity of the mind and the physical activity of the body. The filling of the Spirit (like intoxication) is not a once for all experience. The Christian therefore is daily dependent upon God for empowering by the continuous filling of the Spirit."*

Chafer continues with:

> "To be filled with the Spirit is related to Christian experience, power, and service (bearing fruit.) [The Spirit comes into the life of the believer at salvation, once and for all.] But the filling of the Spirit is a repeated experience and is mentioned frequently in the Bible.
>
> Beginning with the day of Pentecost, a new age dawned in which the Holy Spirit would work in every believer. Now those Christians who had the Spirit of God in them could be filled by the Spirit if he met the conditions. Numerous illustrations in the New Testament confirm this."

He goes on to say:

> "There is an observable difference in the character and quality of the daily life of Christians. Few can be categorized as being full of the Spirit. This lack, however, is not due to failure on the part of God to make provision, but rather failure on the part of the individual to appropriate and permit the Spirit of God to fill his life."

That says it all.

So how does a person walk in the power of the Holy Spirit, where "from his innermost being flows rivers of living water?"

We have to go back to John 7:37. First Jesus says, "If anyone is thirsty" What is thirst? It is an indication of a need. We have to start by approaching God with a sense of neediness. In this time of fear and anxiety, we need to approach Him with this prayer:

> "Lord, I need Your peace in my life."

In one sense, this is an emptying of ourselves so that we may be filled with the Spirit.

So it starts with "If any man is thirsty." Jesus then says, "let him come to Me." We are to go to Him, the source of power, the source of peace that we are seeking. But, how does a person approach God? It starts with humility.

In James 4:8, we are told, "Draw near to God and He will draw near to you. Cleanse your hands you sinners and purify your hearts you double-minded."

In my book, *The Power of a Humble Life*, I wrote about this scripture in James 4:

> *"The book of James gives some insight into the relationship between humility, humbling ourselves, and confession of sin. In James 4:6 we are told God is opposed to the proud but gives grace to the humble. In verse eight, we are told to draw near to God and He will draw near to us. He says that before we can draw near, as sinners we must cleanse our hands and our hearts. We need to cleanse ourselves from not only the outer sins that people see but also the inner sins of the heart. As one commentator put it, 'Your hands and heart symbolize your deeds and thoughts.' Therefore, in order to really draw near to God, we must cleanse ourselves, and this*

> *is done by the confession of sin. Confessing our sin is, as Jesus said, a way we humble ourselves before God."*

It's interesting that, historically, the church would start all worship services with a general confession, where the entire congregation would together confess their sins before God. The intent was to get your heart right as you approached God and prepared for worship.

Finally, in verse 37, Jesus tells us to drink. In I Corinthians 12:13, Paul tells us, "… we were all made to drink of one spirit."

Jesus says in Luke 11:13, "If you then being evil know how to give good gifts to your children, how much more will your heavenly Father give the Holy Spirit to those who ask." Notice this is not asking Christ into your life for salvation. The reason we know this is because you are asking your heavenly Father. This is a Christian asking God his Father to fill him.

Remember, Jesus wants to give us His peace (John 14:27). By faith, we ask Him to fill us with His spirit, and that He would specifically fill us with His peace, one of the fruits of the Spirit. (Galatians 5:22).

When we do this, it's as if God turns on a valve so that His power flows into our lives. It is like the sap of the vine flowing into the branch.

There is only one thing that cuts off the flow of the Spirit, and that is when we sin. John Riddle puts it this way:

> *"The power of the Holy Spirit will continue to flow through us until we sin again. Our sin shuts the valves*

off and the flow stops. The Holy Spirit is still residing in us, but His power is not flowing through us. We are back to operating in the power of the flesh. When we are aware of this, we must go through the steps of re-entering this abiding relationship."

I find myself having to re-enter this abiding relationship throughout the day because of my sinfulness. Yet, I can say this has been a life-changing teaching, dramatically impacting my life over the last 35 years.

EPILOGUE

WATCHING THE news earlier today, I realized the magnitude of uncertainty that exists over the future of this coronavirus. Everyone appeared to be optimistic, as the economy was opening up and the virus seemed to be contained. Then in a brief three-week period, the country experienced a large spike in the virus and, once again, there is so much pending about the future. Will there be a vaccine? If so, when? Will schools reopen and stay open in the fall? If not, how will parents with young children go back to work? Will there be a high school, college and professional sporting events? The questions about our future are many with answers unknown. This is what creates anxiety and fear as we look for certainty. The longer this drags on, the greater the sense of despair and hopelessness we can experience.

Here's the problem. We cannot live with a sense of hopelessness. *The New York Times* featured an article in 2016 about the unfortunate rise in depression and suicide. Robert Putnam, a professor of public policy at Harvard, put his finger on what appears to be at the heart of the problem: hopelessness.

Most of us don't realize we are hope-based creatures. Tim Keller says we underestimate the power of hope in our lives and how much our belief in our future determines how we will live today. We are unavoidably shaped by how we view the future, because it impacts the way we process life in the present—in the now.

Understanding Hope

Before moving forward, we must have a good understanding of hope. In English, the word "hope" is used primarily as a verb and is synonymous with the idea of wishing for something. It is a vague longing for something we don't have, but long for.

However, the word "hope" I am speaking of is a noun and is often used in the Bible. As a noun, it means *a life-shaping certainty of something that has not happened yet, but you know one day will.* It is a very important word in the New Testament and it stresses repeatedly that our relationship with God is the ultimate ground of hope.

Think about it. When you look at a future of uncertainty, and you don't like the possibilities that lay in front of you, you experience a sense of hopelessness, which leads to despair in the now.

Though we may not realize it, we cannot live without hope. Victor Frankl, a Jewish psychiatrist, spoke of this in his famous book, *Man's Search for Meaning*. Frankl was one of the fortunate people to survive the Nazi death camps during World War II. As a trained psychiatrist, he was fascinated as to why some of his fellow prisoners wasted away and died, while others remained strong and survived. He concluded we cannot stay healthy if we don't have hope in the future.

Life in a concentration camp exposes your soul's foundation. Only a few of the prisoners were able to keep their inner liberty and inner strength. Life only has meaning in any circumstances if we have a hope that neither suffering, circumstances, nor death itself can destroy.

Frankl recognized that our believed-in future impacts our ability to live and cope with the hardship of life. If our view of the future is grounded in a solid, ultimate hope, then we have a solid foundation on which to build our lives. However, if our view of the future is rooted in hopelessness, over time we live with an overriding sense of fear and despair.

The Source of Our Hope

Where do we find hope, or who do we look to for hope? As I shared earlier, the Bible stresses repeatedly that our relationship with God is the ultimate ground for hope. Consider the following two verses as they relate to hope.

In the Old Testament, we are told, "For I know the plans I have for you declares the Lord. Plans for welfare, not calamity, to give you a future and a *hope.*" (Jeremiah 29:11) Remember we are future-oriented beings who need to see our lives as purposeful. We are told in this verse in Jeremiah, "I have a plan for you that leads somewhere, that has a purpose."

In previous chapters, we have considered how God uses the storms of life purposefully. They play a part in each of our own stories, leading us to our ultimate good. In the future, we will be able to see how God used this pandemic in each of our lives, helping us to live in peace. It provides hope as we look toward the future.

The second verse relating to hope is Hebrews 6:19 in the New Testament. "We have this hope as an anchor of the soul, firm and secure." In the verse that follows, he reveals that Jesus is the anchor.

What is the anchor of your soul? What is it that you put your hope in? Tim Keller says:

"If you put your ultimate hope in anything in this life, into your job, into money, into your family, into your health, into your status, then suffering and circumstances can take it away, and your life will always be characterized by a ground note of anxiety. You will always be anxious. The only way you are going to be able to face life under any circumstances is if you find a way to put your ultimate hope into something suffering and even death can't take away, something eternal."

There is a hope God calls us to. There is a future He has for us. If we connect our hearts and our lives to it, we will live full and abundant lives, not characterized by fear, because we will have an anchor for our souls.

Our Ultimate Hope

Did you know the ultimate hope of the Christian is Christ's resurrection? In II Corinthians 1:8-10, the Apostle Paul speaks of the affliction and burdens he faced. He felt despair, for the sentence of death was hanging over him. He says the Lord has taught him not to trust in himself, "but in God who raises the dead." He confirms it is "He on whom I have set my hope."

It is important to note that hope is a life-changing certainty that has not happened yet, but we know will. The key phrase here is *life changing*. If you live with hope, it will change your life. It will change the way you see this pandemic. It will change the way you approach the storms of life. And it will change the way you see life's greatest fear: death. We all know death is in our future. At some point, life as we know it today will come to an end.

However, if I know what the final outcome is, and I know it leads to my ultimate good, then I have hope, which enables me to live well in the present as I experience God's peace.

One of my favorite illustrations on hope comes from Philip Yancey. He tells the true story of Americans in a prisoner of war camp in Germany during World War II. They lived in despair with a sense of hopelessness. The prisoners had no idea what the future held for them. They didn't know if Germany was going to win the war, or if they would ever see their families again. There was so much uncertainty.

However, unbeknownst to the guards, the Americans built a makeshift radio. One day, they heard news that the German high command had surrendered, ending the war. Because of a communications breakdown, the German guards didn't yet know. As word spread, a loud celebration broke out.

For three days, the prisoners were hardly recognizable. They sang, waved at guards, laughed at the German shepherds, shared jokes over meals. On the fourth day, they awoke to find that all the Germans had fled, leaving the gates unlocked. The time of waiting had come to an end.

Notice that for three days, their circumstances had not changed. They were still in prison, they were eating the same food, sleeping in the same barracks, being guarded by the same soldiers. Yet, one thing had changed. They knew the final outcome. And that changed everything.

This is how God intends for His people to live, with great joy as we anticipate the future. He has told us what the final outcome is, and what our ultimate destiny is going to be.